Your Amazing
Itty Bitty®

Advanced
Video Marketing
Book

*15 Essential Keys to Becoming a Leader in
Your Industry*

Gary Howarth

Published by Itty Bitty® Publishing
A subsidiary of S & P Productions, Inc.

Printed in the United States of America

Itty Bitty® Publishing
311 Main Street, Suite E
El Segundo, CA 90245
(310) 640-8885

ISBN: 978-1-931191-77-7

To my late wife Terri who was an expert at communicating, staying in touch and making a difference in the world.

Stop by our Itty Bitty™ website to find interesting blog entries regarding Video Marketing

www.IttyBittyPublishing.com

Or visit me at www.zukolt.com.

Table of Contents

Step 1.   Using Video is Easy and Fun
Step 2.   YouTube is the Place to Be
Step 3.   Where is the Best Place to
            "HangOut"?
Step 4.   Facebook and Videos Growing Like
            Crazy
Step 5.   Get Your Emails Opened with Video
Step 6.   iTunes is for More Than Just Music;
            Create Your Own Channel.
Step 7.   Blogs Become Personal
Step 8.   Webinars Never Die, Generate Money
            Anytime
Step 9.   Retain Customers with Personalized
            Video
Step 10.   Bring PowerPoint Presentations to
            Life
Step 11.   Sizzle Reels; Be a Star in Your Niche
Step 12.   No Fancy Equipment Needed
Step 13.   Content is King
Step 14.   Be a Giver
Step 15.   What Do I Say and How Do I Say It?

Simple Steps

Step 1
Using Video is Easy and Fun

Video is the wave of the future. Videos are accessible anywhere, any time. The convenience of smartphones and tablets make creating and posting videos easier than ever. Every day, millions of people are sharing videos on social media platforms like Facebook, YouTube, LinkedIn, and Twitter, to name a few. Most people, given a choice of reading a letter or watching a video, will go with the video.

1. YouTube processes more than 3 billion searches a month.
2. Today's audiences prefer video (instant gratification).
3. Effective means of promoting events.
4. Use for information purposes to generate trust and confidence in you.
5. Create press release messages.
6. Makes a great introduction to your product.

Why You Should Use Video

- In a study by the University of Pennsylvania in 1970, researchers discovered that only 7% of our communication is the words that we say (content).
- 38% of our communication is the tonality, which includes: tone of voice, timbre, tempo and volume.
- 55% is non-verbal communication, such as: facial expressions, body posture, breathing and movement.
- Matching the verbal and non-verbal communication is what creates trust, rapport and a level of congruency. These are the things that will grow your business.
- Excellent way to express emotion and generate emotion within your client base.
- If a picture is worth a 1000 words, then a video is worth a million words and tells the whole story.
- Video works well where it matches the markets/viewers to their needs/expectations.
- Video creates experiences that are memorable, moving and inspiring. These experiences provide awareness and eventual sales.

Step 2
YouTube is the Place to Be

YouTube is the number one source of videos in the world with over 4-billion views every day! Here are key things you need to know to get the most out of what YouTube has to offer.

1. Create a YouTube Channel and make sure all the content is consistent and follows a common theme.
2. The video descriptions must include keywords related to your subject. Tag and title your videos appropriately, and be specific.
3. Include your URL at the beginning and end of the video, to drive the viewers to your website.
4. Use annotations (speech bubbles, pop up boxes for notes, titles, labels to name a specific part of your video) in your video to enhance the message, but do it sparingly. They work really well to generate sales and leads.
5. Make your videos public and allow comments to maximize exposure.
6. Place an End Card (interactive outro) at the end of your videos to drive viewers to your website, social media pages and a link to allow them to subscribe to your YouTube channel.

How to Make the Most from YouTube Videos

- Write compelling titles and descriptions while using appropriate keywords. With the right keywords and tags, your content is optimized and the probability of your videos being found with YouTube and Google searches are maximized.
- In your YouTube channel, assign featured content, organize videos into playlists and groups and add subscribers to your feed.
- Promote your business focused videos with YouTube TrueView ads.
- Utilize YouTube Cards so your destination URL, title, and call-to-action text can be accessed on mobile devices as well as desktop.
  - The best YouTube Card for driving leads and sales for your business is an "Associated Website Card," which links directly to your associated website.

Step 3
Where is the Best Place to "HangOut"?

Google Hangouts is designed to be "the future" (Google says so) of messaging service. A great feature is video conferencing. Why would you want to use Google Hangouts?

1. Video Conferences allow up to nine people that can interact with each other.
2. Your video conference streams live in HD and is automatically saved to your YouTube channel.
3. Meet face-to-face with customers and coworkers.
4. Broadcast live events to demo a new product or make an announcement. The broadcasts can go live in HD on Google+, YouTube and your website.
5. It will be recorded and automatically saved on your YouTube channel.
6. Hangouts have no time limit and you can use Hangouts OnAir to broadcast a Hangout to as many people as you like.
7. During the video conference, you can share your screen. This lets you show them pictures, graphics, charts, or anything else that will support your presentation

Ways to Utilize Hangouts in Your Business

- Share a topic with the world. You can stream a conference keynote or moderate a panel discussion with experts.
- Hold live video meetings with your customers to improve communications and reduce cycle time – great for sharing new products.
- Have virtual meetings for trainings to save time and travel expenses, yet get all the benefits of face-to-face contact. They can even be recorded for viewing again.
- Conduct interviews with employment candidates or with industry leaders.

Step 4
Facebook and Videos Growing Like Crazy

Facebook has 4 billion video views per day. Uploading videos directly into Facebook provides better appearance than linking a YouTube video to your post. Mobile video ads are an excellent opportunity for businesses to brand themselves. It is time to get on the bandwagon.

1. Facebook makes it easy for users to integrate video into their Facebook pages and posts.
2. Utilize auto-play with Facebook native videos (native videos are uploaded directly into Facebook, not as a link from YouTube).
3. Native videos give you an option to add a Call-To-Action button at the end of the video, so you direct the viewers who watched the whole video to a specific URL.
4. Native videos also display the number of views the video received.
5. You can tag people in your Facebook videos, which increases interaction.

Facebook Video Ads are Effective for Branding

- Facebook averages more than 1 billion video views every day.
- More than 65% of Facebook video views happen on mobile devices.
- Mobile equates to mass media and the branding message easily reaches people who have their devices on 24/7.
- Use inspirational videos to get more shares and exposure to your brand.
- Use stories in your videos that come from the heart, especially effective for non-profits.
- Teach something useful that your audience would like.
- Keep the video short and place a link in the description to drive traffic to your site.
- Create playlists for each target market, so there is a natural progression though your videos that makes sense to them.
- Get multiple uses from your videos by embedding them in your blog posts. The videos play in the blogpost and viewers see all the comments and interaction on the post.

Step 5
Get Your Emails Opened with Video

Email is one of the most common methods of communicating with prospects and clients. In business it is used for intra-company communications, marketing purposes and coordinating with business partners, suppliers and customers. Up and coming generations of workers are more comfortable using email than traditional letters or memos. Now there are services that embed videos into emails, increasing their effectiveness.

1. When a recipient sees that there is a video in the subject line, open rates increase 13%. More people will see your message.
2. With videos in your emails, you are combining sight, sound and motion. This combination increases the level of communication so people can relate to you.
3. Video emails increase trust and rapport.
4. Video emails are perfect for personal messages that you want to remain private. No need to post on public sites like YouTube, Facebook and Twitter.

Advantages of Using Video in Emails

- Websites like www.Zukolt.com make it easy with the equipment you already have - laptop, tablets or smartphones.
- With www.Zukolt.com you can schedule when you want a video to be delivered, allowing you to build email campaigns.
- Video emails provide you the flexibility to shape the content towards specific demographics and customer profiles for maximum impact.
- Easily customize and personalize the video for a specific customer or group of customers.
- Maintain privacy for personalized videos.

Types of Email Videos to Create

- Thank you videos for customers.
- Follow up video after networking events.
- Use videos to promote upcoming events of webinars.
- Include videos focusing on specific products, services and updates.
- Recognition of birthdays and anniversaries.
- Appointment reminders.
- And many more……

Step 6
i-Tunes is for More Than Just Music
Create Your Own Channel

iTunes channels are dedicated links for video podcasts you create for your business. Video podcasting helps build businesses. It enables you to promote your products and services in cost effective ways. Steps to start an iTunes channel:

1. Create your video podcast and export it to Apple iTunes in a compatible file format—MOV and MP4 video files.
2. Create an iTunes account.
3. The iTunes Store provides brief summaries of the podcasts, so it is important to include as much metadata as possible in the ID tags for your file. When people are browsing for new channels to subscribe to, this is part of searchable content.
4. Upload your video podcast to the Web. This can be your own website. The hosting service for your website must provide RSS feed capabilities.
5. Open the iTunes app on your computer, open the Podcasts directory and click "Submit a Podcast."
6. Enter your podcast and RSS feed address. Then iTunes will notify you within 24 hours when your podcast is accepted.

Video Podcasts are a Great Way to Share Information and Should be Repurposed.

- They should be used in conjunction with your website and YouTube.
- Video podcasts are also being used for web television (Web TV).
- As an alternative to iTunes, Spotify announced it is adding non-music to its app. If your clients are regular users of Spotify, this could be an option for you.
- Transcribe your podcast and include it in your blog.
- Video Podcasts are great for interviewing guests who are of interest to your market. If you can't be in the same room, recording with GoToMeeting, along with Skype, is effective.
- The podcasts can be posted on LinkedIn and other social media platforms.
- Other Podcasters to consider in addition to iTunes for distribution of your Podcast are Banshee, Clementine, Juice, NewsFire and Stitcher.

Step 7
Blogs Become Personal

A video blog, or vlog, is a form of blog that uses video as the medium. The best way to maximize customer interest in your vlog is to combine video, supporting text and images. Anyone with a video capable camera (including smartphones or iPhones) and an up-to-date computer with a high-speed connection and editing software can create a vlog, and publish and distribute it online. Here are some keys to consider when creating a vlog.

1. Identify your target audience.
2. Decide on a topic that is relevant and interesting to your audience.
3. Write out a rough draft of a script and follow it. The script should not be repeated word for word to give it a more personal feel.
4. Decide where you are going to record and set up the lighting and background. Dress appropriately.
5. Begin recording and film several takes.
6. Process your recording through a movie editing program with software, such as Windows Movie Maker or iMovie, if you have a Mac. Here you can add titles, credits, music and random effects.

Other Considerations When Publishing Your Video Blog (Vlog)

- Find a web host for your video blog. There are free web services such as YouTube or Vimeo that will host your videos.
- You should create your own blog website through Wordpress or another service for embedding your videos.
- Your vlog needs a title that is catchy and easy to remember so it can attract repeat viewers.
- Develop enough content so you can keep going for a while. Frequent vlogs with new content will hold your audience's interest and keep them checking in.
- A frequently updated vlog increases your web presence and attracts potential customers.
- Improve the visibility of your vlogs by adding strong titles, tags and descriptions.
- Assemble and post other people's videos that will be of interest to your audience (get permission first).
- Promote your vlog through social media and send out an email to all your contacts with a link to the vlog.

Step 8
Webinars Never Die
Generate Money Anytime

Webinars are known as either web conferencing or seminars on the web. A great advantage to using webinars is to generate leads for your business because participants can come from all over the world. Webinars are a fantastic marketing tool and sales generator. It is possible to rerun a webinar multiple times to engage as many people as possible and you only need to create the original live version one time. Reasons to run a webinar are:

1. Convenience for viewers. They can participate without having to leave their home.
2. Uniquely designed as an effective method for education and training. Viewers can ask questions and interact with the host.
3. Inexpensive, saving on travel costs for face-to-face seminars Services like Goggle+ Hangouts on Air are free.
4. Can help you grow your contact list. By having guests on your webinars that offer something special to your market, you are introduced to their contact lists as well.

Action Items for a Successful Webinar

- Determine whether a free service like Google+ Hangouts on Air will meet your needs or use a service like GoToWebinar or ClickWebinar to host the webinar that offers many more services.
- Focus on giving good information during the body of the webinar and in the last 5 minutes, promote your product and give them a call to action.
- Give yourself several weeks to prepare for the webinar, including pre-webinar promotion.
  - Promotion methods include: talking about it in your blogs, sending emails to your list 1 month before, 3 weeks before, 1 week before and 1 day before. Place notifications on your website and add social media notifications.
- Follow up with participants after the webinar by sending them additional materials, a link to the recording, and anything new you have going including related content on your website and upcoming events. Put the recording on your website to track future activity.

Step 9
Retain Customers with Personalized Video

Customers get upset when they see you marketing for new customers, when you don't bother to stay in frequent contact with them. Don't ignore them! Remember that existing customers pay for everything (especially the top 20%), including your marketing to new prospects. Most customers leave because they feel you are indifferent to them. There are things you can do to retain customers.

1. Send them a video email so they remember your face and voice. Use it for any updates or new products you have that would be beneficial to them.
2. Go out of your way to give over-the-top customer service.
3. With video email, how you feel about your customers comes through because they can see it in your face and hear it in your voice.
4. In your message to your customers, make sure that you are accessible to them. That is part of showing that you care.

More Ways to Retain Your Customers

- Under-promise and over-deliver.
- In your communications, make sure your customers feel appreciated. Make a special offer just to them for being loyal.
- Never offer something to new prospects that you are not willing to give to your existing customers.
- Listen to your customers and give them what they want, instead of insisting on offering what you have. Be open and adapt to their needs.
- Never let your communications with customers become boring or routine. Be unique and send video emails and use video blogs to connect with them.
- Finally, be grateful for your customers because they can choose to spend their money somewhere else. It is up to you.

Step 10
Bring PowerPoint Presentations to Life

Video in PowerPoint can complement the idea of a presentation or slide immediately. It increases the impact of the message being delivered. The segments must be of high quality and used properly in order to generate the appropriate emotion in your audience. Each Video must contribute to the primary point of your presentation. Presentations with too much text can lose the audience. Keep them engaged with video.

1. When you include video in your presentation, you can choose to either play when you click the play button, or start automatically when you reach the slide where the video is embedded.

2. Videos can either be embedded in your presentation or included as a link.

3. The most reliable method is to choose to embed the video. It creates a larger total file size, but eliminates the possibility of a link breaking. A link breaking can happen if a network servicer isn't available or your internet connection is weak or unavailable.

More Considerations for Using Video in Your PowerPoint Presentation

- If you want to use only a portion of a video you want to include in your presentation, PowerPoint has features that will allow you to:
  - Trim the start and end of a video.
  - Automatically start the video upon entering the slide in a slideshow view.
  - Set the video to play full screen.
- The supported file formats are MPEG-4 files (.mp4), QuickTime (.mov.qt), Windows Video file (.avi), Movie file (.mpg or mpeg), Windows Media Video file (.wmv), and Adobe Flash Media (.swf).
- The size and quality of the video file is determined by the resolution. Select a high enough resolution, so people can see it from the back of the room.
- Get permission to use videos that you did not create yourself or do not own. It will avoid future legal issues.
- Using a video editing tool like Camtasia allows you to make a video of a PowerPoint presentation, including narration, for when you are unable to appear at the presentation.

Step 11
Sizzle Reels; Be a Star in Your Niche

Sizzle reels are fast-paced, 3 to 5 minute videos that combine audio, visuals and messaging to provide an overview of your brand, product or service. They are used for sales and marketing presentations, introductions, and on your website. Speakers, authors and coaches, to name a few, use sizzle reels to make an impression on their audience. Business people need a high-impact sizzle reel that accurately tells their message, fascinates their audience and leaves a positive impression.

1. Appeal to the audience's emotions rather than their intellect. You want to propel the audience to take action.
2. Emotions are the fuel that will send your messages soaring.
3. Combine music with your sizzle reel to keep the viewers engaged and trigger positive emotions for you. It is critical to know your audience and what they will respond to whether the music is upbeat and fun, or serious and reassuring.
4. Sizzle reels should be a combination of high quality video clips, high definition photographs, a small amount of text messages, and motivational music.

Sizzle Reels Are Tricky

- Poorly created sizzle reels can turn prospects off to your message and brand.
- Use the highest quality audio, video and photo assets possible.
- Your sizzle reel must be five-star, or better left undone.
- Ensure that you own all the rights to the content you use.
- Be concise in your message and keep it short. You are only giving a sample of your offering, whether it is a product, service, or you.
- Include testimonials, if appropriate, to support your message.
- Keep in mind how your message will benefit your audience. Focus on their needs and desires.
- Consider using a professional videographer that specializes in sizzle reels, for maximum impact and speed.

Step 12
No Fancy Equipment Needed

There are only a few basic items you need to create video content and share it. The essentials are an HD video camera, high quality mic, stabilization device, lighting, computer and editing software. The key to any video is great quality sound. If the sound is poor, even if the video portion is great, it leaves a poor impression. When you are creating video to promote your business, brand, or educating, you need to look as professional as possible.

1. Smartphones can make professional quality video now. It is the least expensive way to get started. If you choose this route, you must add a lapel, or lavalier microphone. Also, shaky hand shots typically look amateurish. Use a cell phone tripod adapter, available for less than $10 on Amazon. Connect this to a tripod for better results.

2. Lavalier microphones are excellent for recording speech and dialog. As you are utilizing the video marketing suggestions recommended in this book, the majority will fall in this category.

3. If you want to look professional, lighting is a key. There are lighting kits available from Amazon at relatively low prices.

Additional Equipment and Tips to Look Like a Pro

- A substantial tripod will always make your videos more professional.
- Video editing software is essential. I use Camtasia which allows me to control the audio track in addition to adding intros and outros to my videos, add logos and text, and special effects. This allows you control over how your video looks and sounds.
- Use a camera with high image quality. Look for a camera with 1080p for the best quality. DSLR's are a great way to go and you can change lenses depending upon what you're recording.
- No matter what kind of camera you select, great sound is a requirement. Your audience expects professional sound with a professional looking video. Utilize lavalier microphones. Shotgun microphones also provide excellent sound but are more expensive. When I don't connect my microphone to the recording device, I use a Tascam Linear PCM Recorder so I can move freely while recording. Then I use Camtasia to sync my audio with the video.
- Finally, practice and see what works best for you.

Step 13
Content is King

Now we know that video is going to make a significant difference in your business. The question now is, "What topics will I share in my videos?" More to the point, "What does my audience care about?" Ideas for videos are the same as ideas for blogging. Here are a few ideas to get the little grey cells working.

1. Company updates to keep the audience informed about your company's services, products and projects.
2. Keep your customers in mind and create videos related to hot trends in your industry that will affect them.
3. Offer instructional videos showing customers how to use the products and services you provide. (Think 'how-to' videos.)
4. Employee bios and introductions are always engaging. It brings a human element to your company. It helps prospects feel more comfortable buying your product or service.
5. Ask your clients and community what questions they have or what information they want. Answering their questions builds rapport.

More Content Ideas

- Interviews of experts in your field and related industries are a great way to share really valuable content without you needing to come up with it on your own.
- Customer testimonials related to a product or service that you want to highlight. It is always good to share independent opinions of your offerings. Include client success stories.
- Video provides a medium to explain the details of what you are offering and linking a human face to your business.
- Behind the scenes videos that show your audience how you do business.
- Answers to FAQs. If you receive the same questions repeatedly, that is a good topic for a video.
- Tie current events to your products or services and share how it will impact your audience. If there is a topic that everyone is talking about, it is a great opportunity to add value to the discussion.
- Ask yourself, what keeps your customers awake at night? They would love ideas that would solve those problems.
- Tell a story related to your topic. Everyone loves stories.

Step 14
Be a Giver

A giver is someone that is focused on another person's needs and is willing to spend the time and effort helping others. Sometimes it is at the expense of personal gain, but in the long-run it can result in gaining trust, generating credibility, establishing relationships and creating rapport. It is important to keep this in mind when you are putting together your videos.

1. There is an old saying that goes, "When clients know you, like you, and trust you, they will buy from you."

2. Giving great content and making the personal connection in your videos allows the audience to get to know you, like you and trust you.

3. Don't be afraid of giving too much. Offer solutions to their most urgent problems and challenges. They will appreciate it and want to do business with you.

4. Today, with the arrival of social media, videos must be more interactive with your prospects and clients. Research what concerns them and address it in your videos. Give them a couple of different ways to contact you, so the discussion can continue.

How to Create Content From a Giver's Perspective

- Always make the videos mostly about the prospects and a little about you and your business. Here you can tie in how you can help them resolve their problems and challenges.
- Present yourself in an honest, straight-forward and authentic way to make a deeper connection with your audience.
- Think about how you can provide tremendous value while helping your prospects and clients.
- Consider your videos as delivering the best possible experience.

Step 15
What Do I Say and How Do I Say It?

Videos are powerful because the elements of
communication are 7% the words we say, 38%
tonality, and 55% is physiology. That is why
video is a fantastic way to communicate when
you can't be there in person. Your audience
experiences all of it. Even though words only
make up 7%, it is still important. To
communicate most effectively, here are a few
suggestions based on tried and true sales
techniques.

1. Use words that will connect people who
   are visual, auditory and kinesthetic. For a
   visual audience, use phrases like, "looks
   good" and "paint a picture." For auditory
   people, use phrases like, "clear as a bell"
   and "sounds good." "Feels good" and
   "get a hold of" resonate with kinesthetic
   people.

2. Rate of speech is also vital. Visual people
   typically talk fast and kinesthetic people
   talk slow and purposeful. Vary your rate
   or speech to ensure that everyone is
   engaged with what you are saying.

3. Varying the volume of your voice is
   another technique to keep your audience
   from falling asleep. Never be monotone,
   use inflection in your voice.

Tips on Being Compelling

- The viewer of your video wants certain things. The desire for them is the dominant idea in their mind all the time. Tune in on their dominant thoughts, and you have their attention. Connect it with your offer and they will be interested.
- Arouse the feeling or emotions in your audience so they must have whatever you are offering.
- Use word pictures that are so clear that your audience can almost see what you are offering. Help them visualize your proposition.
- Use proof in your videos. Testimonials from customers help dispel doubt in a hesitant prospect.
- In a sales video, once you have given them all the reasons they should accept your offer, then arouse in them the fear that they will lose something worthwhile if they don't act. It acts like a hook.
- To summarize, your sales videos should include a description or explanation, the motive or reason why they should buy, the proof or guarantee, the penalty for not buying, and the close, which tells the audience what to do.

You've finished. Before you go…

Tweet/share that you finished this book.
Please star rate this book.
Reviews are solid gold to writers. Please
take a few minutes to give us some itty
bitty feedback on this book.

ABOUT THE AUTHOR

Having been in sales and marketing to Fortune 100 companies for over 35 years, I learned a few things along the way. One thing I learned was that if I was selling to IBM, Boeing, or the new start up down the street, they all had one thing in common: effective communication with individuals. At the end of the day, all sales are to individuals, no matter who they work for.

Even though I went to school for my MBA, I learned much more from doing. Since communication is the key to all success in life, I decided, along with my nephew, to start a video email marketing business called Zukolt. We took a boring medium and made it interesting again.

I always had an interest in Neuro Linguistic Programming (NLP) because it is all about how we communicate and how the brain functions. I am a certified NLP Practitioner and incorporated some of the training in this book in order to provide you with a broader view of communicating.

I am creating a workshop based on this book to provide more detail about how to actually do some of the things I recommend. The video email website is www.zukolt.com. My personal website is www.garyhowarth.com.

If You Enjoyed This Book
You Might Also Enjoy…

- **Your Amazing Itty Bitty® Travel Planning Book** – Rosemary Workman
- **Your Amazing Itty Bitty® Little Black Book of Sales** – Anthony Comacho
- **Your Amazing Itty Bitty® Safety Book** – Stephen C. Carpenter, CSP

With many more Amazing Itty Bitty® books available in paperback or digital form.